The Least You Should Know About Meditation

A Brief and Practical Guide To Mindfulness

Mac MacLean

Riley Publishing
Victoria, British Columbia, Canada

ISBN: 978-06921622-2-4

Don't just do something. Sit there.

Table of Contents

Introduction

To meditate, you must be able to:

— Count from 1 to 10

— Breathe

— Sit still for a few minutes

Assuming that you can manage these tasks, you can learn to meditate.

But even though you already have all the necessary skills, learning to meditate is not easy. Meditation involves changing some thought patterns of a lifetime, and so learning to meditate requires patience and persistence. This guide will help you to make that effort by explaining in plain English, without exotic terms or concepts, the *least* you should know about meditation. And the least you should know includes not only *how* to meditate, but also *why* you are meditating.

Because meditation has been practiced for thousands of years in many different cultures and religious traditions, there are countless varieties of meditation. The type of meditation described here—a form of mindfulness meditation—is one type of practice among many. It is not the only way to meditate; it is simply a good place to start. And the steps suggested here are not chiseled in stone or divinely inspired; experiment and adapt them to fit your needs.

Meditation can change how you experience and deal with the realities of your life.

Meditation will not magically transform your life. It won't make you smarter or younger or funnier or richer. But meditation can change how you experience and deal with the realities of your life by helping you to focus on the present and control the mental "noise" of distracting thoughts.

Learning to meditate is not quick or easy. But, as countless people over many centuries have learned, meditation can be well worth the effort. Since meditation doesn't require expensive equipment, lots of time, or strenuous physical effort, why not give it a try?

Why Meditate?

A well respected meditation teacher writes:

> *"...meditation can help us fulfill our deepest desires, to discover inner freedom and happiness and to come to a sense of oneness with life.... The practice helps us to discover what the whole process of life and death is about."*

Such cosmic benefits are unlikely to result from the meditation practice described here. But the simple meditation practice outlined in this guide can be of great value, on several different levels.

A Quieter Mind

> *"There are many varieties of meditation, but what they generally have in common are techniques for making the mind peaceful."*
>
> —*The Dalai Lama*

At the very least, the meditation practice described in this guide offers periods of mental quiet, of respite from the concerns which normally bombard our minds. It is unlikely that there is anyone who would not benefit from such interludes.

"The incessant stream of thoughts flowing through our minds leaves us very little respite for inner quiet.... We get caught up in the torrent and it winds up submerging our lives as it carries us to places we may not wish to go and may not even realize we are headed for.

Meditation means learning how to get out of this current, sit by its bank and listen to it, learn from it, and then use its energies to guide us rather than to tyrannize us."

— Jon Kabat-Zinn

Being in the Moment

A more subtle benefit of meditation is learning to be attuned to the present, or to be "in the moment." Although that over-used phrase may sound like jargon, the concept is not just psycho-babble.

At the risk of stating the obvious, the present is fundamentally different from the past or the future. The past and the future are obviously important, and our awareness of them is part of what makes us human. But the past and future, even though they have happened or will happen, currently exist only in our minds. The only actual reality going on now is the present.

> *"The past is already gone, yet we cling to it. The future is not yet here, but we dwell on it. Even when we talk about now, the now we are talking about is already gone."*
>
> —*Taizan Maezumi Roshi*

Meditation is not, of course, the only way to be in the moment. We all have times when our attention is fully focused on the present: watching a particularly exciting sports event, trying to figure out a new smartphone app, or enjoying an ocean view. But meditation gives us practice in focusing on the present, making it easier for us to be "in the moment" when we are not meditating.

Why should we care about focusing on the present—being in the moment? Because the present, whether joyful or distressing, is what we have to deal with now. And too often, our ability to deal with our present reality (whether an event or an emotion or a problem) is hampered by the intrusion of wandering thoughts concerning the past or future.

By helping us to learn how to focus on the present, meditation helps us deal directly and clearly with whatever realities— good or bad—we are facing.

Research on the Effects of Meditation

Many recent studies have examined the mental and physical effects of meditation. These studies seem to confirm what meditators have long recognized: that meditation is good for us in a variety of ways. Studies on the effects of meditation include:

— In a January 2014 article in *Clinical Psychology Review*, based on an examination of 209 prior studies, researchers concluded that mindfulness meditation is an especially effective treatment for reducing anxiety, depression and stress.

— Since meditation involves focused attention, it is not surprising that many studies have shown that meditation strengthens a person's ability to sustain attention on a particular object.

— A study reported in *The Harvard Gazette* found that eight weeks of meditation caused measurable decreases in the density of the area of the brain associated with stress.

— Several brain-scan studies have concluded that meditation strengthens areas of the brain involving memory, learning, and emotional flexibility.

— The November 2014 issue of *Scientific American* reported that meditation produces changes to the brain, which enables people to withstand stress better and to react more quickly to certain types of stimuli.

— The same *Scientific American* issue noted several studies that have documented mindfulness meditation reducing symptoms of anxiety and depression and improving sleep patterns.

Our Wandering Minds

Our minds tend to wander. A lot. Unless we are experiencing a particularly intense event or emotion, our minds receive a continuous stream of random thoughts: recollections of past events, concerns for the future, etc. Because we are so used to our minds wandering, we generally don't realize how frequent and persistent such random thoughts are—how often we are thinking about things other than what is happening right now.

Almost half our waking thoughts have little relation to what we are currently doing

A frequently cited study by Harvard University psychologists analyzed responses to random smartphone inquiries to 2,250 participants asking what they were doing and what they were thinking about. Based on the responses, the study concluded that the mind's default mode is "mind wandering," and that almost half our waking thoughts have little relation to what we are currently doing.

Meditation does not seek the impossible and undesirable goal of permanently banishing all wandering thoughts from our minds. Meditation simply teaches us how to exercise a bit more control over our thoughts than we are used to.

"What we hope to learn is the difference between thinking and being lost in thought. We don't want to stop our thoughts but to change our relationship with them—to be more present and aware when we're thinking. If we're aware of what we're thinking, if we see clearly what is going on in our minds, then we can choose whether and how to act on our thoughts."

—Sharon Salzberg

When meditating, we are mentally turning away from the continuous stream of wandering thoughts which tend to occupy our minds. Instead, during meditation we focus on something that is happening right now—our breathing—while counting and noting the physical sensation of our breaths.

But if a goal of meditation is to clear our mind, however temporarily, of distracting wandering thoughts, why should we add to our mental clutter by counting our breaths? Why not just clear our minds and skip the breath counting?

The best way to answer this question is to do a brief experiment. Find a clock or smartphone app which will tell you when 30 seconds have passed. Now try to avoid having any thoughts whatsoever during that half minute. START NOW.

The odds are that well before 30 seconds had passed, some wandering thoughts will have crossed your mind. Not thinking about anything for any length of time turns out to be extraordinarily difficult.

Now make two changes to this brief mental experiment. First, hold your breath during the entire 30 seconds. Second, stare intently at some object during the 30 seconds. Again, try to avoid having any thoughts during the half-minute, but this time while also holding your breath and staring intently at something. START NOW.

Holding your breath and staring may not have kept random thoughts entirely out of your mind, but you probably had better luck in keeping your mind clear than before you added those steps. The reason, of course, is that the modest mental effort you expended in holding your breath and staring at something gave your mind something—admittedly not much—to do, making your mind less receptive to the usual stream of wandering thoughts.

Since holding your breath for an entire meditation period isn't possible, in this meditation practice we give our minds some equally undemanding tasks: noticing the physical sensations of our breathing while counting our breaths. This minimal mental activity provides some necessary mental "filler" which will help keep wandering thoughts at bay during meditation.

But before discussing breath counting further, we'll look at the preliminary question of how to sit for meditation.

Sitting Meditation Positions

Meditation can be practiced in many different ways: walking meditation, eating meditation, sleeping meditation (really), etc. But the most common form is sitting meditation, and that is what is described here.

Although you might think that sitting mediation will require you to sit in some particular (probably uncomfortable) manner, that is not so. The only requirements for sitting meditation are that you be sitting and that you be alert. So you have options.

You can meditate while sitting on a chair, while sitting on the floor, or while kneeling on the floor (which, admittedly, isn't really sitting). All are perfectly appropriate positions for meditating. What matters in meditation is what goes on in your head, not how you arrange your legs.

Your Back

Whether you meditate sitting on a chair, sitting on the floor, or kneeling, getting your back into a stable and comfortable position and keeping it there is the most important physical part of meditation. The point of good posture isn't for appearance—no style points are awarded in meditation. Rather, good meditation posture, neither slouching nor ramrod tense, will help to avoid the distraction of an aching back.

On a chair or a cushion or a bench, the posture for the upper part of your body is the same: upright and attentive, without being uncomfortably rigid. Bring the small of your back and your belly a bit forward, and pull your shoulders a bit back.

As you meditate, you'll probably need to correct your posture—generally by straightening up—from time to time.

A good way to adjust your posture during meditation is to imagine that your head is touching the ceiling; stretch upward to have the top of your head raise the imaginary ceiling for a few seconds, and then relax slightly into an attentive posture.

Sitting on a Chair

For meditating while sitting on a chair, choose one with a firm seat rather than your most comfortable armchair or couch. Your goal is to meditate, not to snooze. Place both feet on the floor (putting something underneath your feet if necessary for support). Sit forward on the chair with your back straight and without resting against the back.

Sitting on a chair is so familiar that it requires no mental or physical effort. But the familiarity of a chair is also a disadvantage; it can make the meditation experience seem so ordinary that meditation may lose some of its special character. So if you feel physically up to it, at least experiment with sitting on the floor or kneeling to meditate.

Sitting on the Floor

The most common meditation posture involves sitting on the floor. Since most of us are not used to sitting on the floor for any length of time, sitting on the floor will get uncomfortable very quickly without the aid of something that will soften the contact between you and the floor. Meditation mats and cushions serve that purpose.

Meditation Mats and Cushions

You can improvise a mat from things on hand. But if you are going to make a serious effort to meditate, you will benefit from having a mat intended especially for meditation. A meditation mat—sometimes referred to by the Japanese term *zabuton*—is generally about 2 feet by 3 feet, although bigger mats are available for especially tall people.

You may be able to improvise around the need for a meditation mat, but getting a cushion designed for meditation is probably essential for reasonable comfort in any of the sitting postures (and for some kneeling postures). By sitting on the cushion you raise your body above the level of the mat, making it easier to arrange your legs in any of the sitting postures described below. A meditation cushion—sometimes referred to by the Japanese term *zafu*— is typically about a foot diameter. The most common form of meditation cushion looks like a puffed up Frisbee, and is several inches high.

An alternative style of meditation cushion looks more like a cross section of a cylinder and, crucially, is as much as 8 inches high. The extra height of this style of cushion, which one website calls a "hi-zafu," is important: the higher you are off the ground, the easier it will be to arrange your legs in any of the sitting postures, and a more substantial cushion will provide more support for a kneeling posture.

For all of the meditation positions involving sitting on the floor, set the cushion toward the back of the mat. Then sit on the forward part of the cushion so that the weight of your body is distributed between your behind and your legs or knees. It is essential that your legs/knees bear part of your weight. That triangle distribution of weight will give you the most stability and (after some practice) comfort while you meditate.

Mats and cushions are sold on numerous websites, including dharmacrafts. com and zafustore.com. Both are available in a variety of colors, but black is your best choice as the traditional color. Choose buckwheat hull filling.

Buying a cushion and mat together is usually a good idea, and should reduce the price slightly. The combination should run a bit over $100 US.

If you are already buying a mat and cushion you may also want to get a pair of small extra cushions which can provide support if your legs aren't supple enough for your knees to reach the mat in one of the sitting positions.

Cross-Legged Position

The easiest floor sitting position for most people, at least initially, is cross-legged. Unfortunately, sitting cross-legged can get uncomfortable pretty quickly, and isn't particularly stable.

Burmese Position

A preferable alternative to the cross-legged position is called the Burmese position: move your ankles so that the heels are close together and directly in front of you. Bring your knees down as close to the mat as you can without discomfort. If you have extremely supple legs, the sides of your calves will touch the mat, putting you in a stable tripod base, consisting of your behind (resting on the forward portion of the cushion) and the sides of your calves. But for most of us, our legs won't readily go flat without great strain—don't try to force them—so you may want to put a small pillow under each knee to give enough support to approximate a tripod base.

Quarter Lotus Position

Another alternative to the cross-legged position, called the Quarter Lotus, provides stability and reasonable comfort for those who can manage it. For the Quarter Lotus, the heel of one foot is brought close to the body (or cushion), and the other foot is placed on the calf of the opposing leg. Your knees will point to the corners of the mat and will (ideally) be on the mat to provide stability. Lean forward slightly so that your knees and calves bear part of your weight. If you have trouble getting your knees down to the mat, small cushions under one or both knees can provide stability.

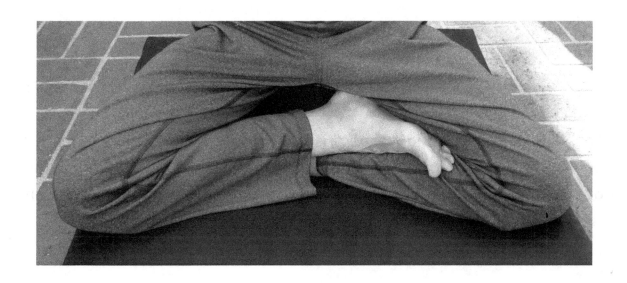

Half-Lotus Position

The Half-Lotus (as you might expect) is a step up in difficulty from the Quarter Lotus, and requires more than the usual flexibility. One foot is placed on the opposing thigh, while the other foot rests mostly on the ground. This position isn't easy for most of us. Don't try to force it.

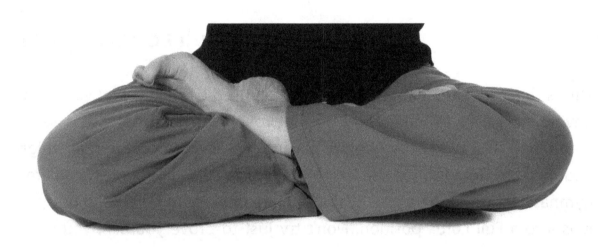

Full Lotus Position

This is the iconic meditation sitting position used by monks and yogis who devote their lives to meditation, and it provides the most stable base for meditation. The Full Lotus involves placing the left foot on the right thigh, and then the right foot on the left thigh (or vice versa). But unless you are a gymnast or have done a lot of yoga, you are unlikely to be able to get your legs into a Full Lotus position. Don't try just to prove you can; you could injure your legs and knees.

Kneeling

A kneeling position for meditation is more challenging than sitting on a chair, but less demanding than sitting on the floor. To meditate while kneeling, you will want to have a mat to protect your knees from the hard floor unless you are on a very soft carpet.

One possible posture for kneeling meditation is to rest your weight on your heels. But this posture is unlikely to remain comfortable for long.

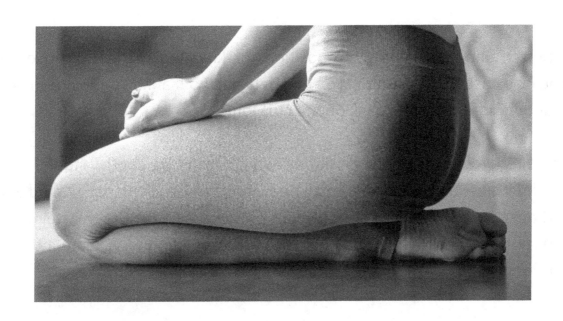

A better, and more common, position for kneeling meditation involves placing a cushion (or cushions) on end between your ankles and underneath your behind, and sitting back on the cushion(s).

An alternative kneeling position—which can be both stable and comfortable—makes use of a small tilted wooden bench placed behind you and over your ankles. You then sit back on the bench to take the weight of your body off your heels. Such benches are available on the same internet vendor websites as mats and cushions.

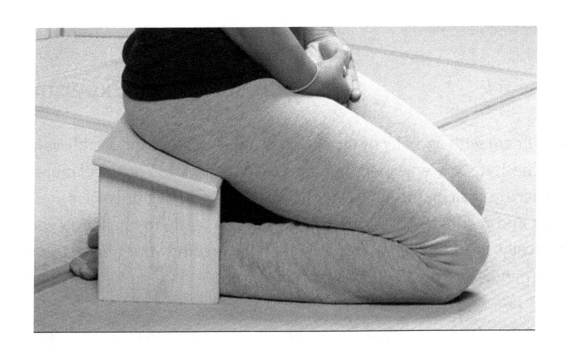

Experiment

Experiment with as many of the sitting options as you comfortably can, and don't hesitate to keep experimenting. On some days you may feel more agile and decide to sit on the floor. On other days you may decide to give your legs a rest and meditate while sitting in a chair. Be ready to challenge yourself physically, but without having discomfort overcome your ability to have a quiet mind.

Other Meditation Logistics

Hands

Your hands have to go somewhere, and dangling them at your sides would be a distraction. Regardless of how you are sitting, one obvious possible location for your hands is on your thighs, with your palms up or down.

A slightly more ambitious approach, sometimes used in yoga, is to rest your hands, palms up, on your knees, and bring the thumb and the index finger (or the middle finger) of each hand together to form a circle.

A different approach, in the Zen tradition, involves putting your right hand (palm up) on your lap, and putting your left hand (palm up) on top of your right so that the middle knuckles overlap. Then lightly bring the tips of your thumbs together, so that your fingers and thumbs form an oval shape.

Try different hand positions, and see what feels natural and comfortable. Choosing a position for your hands is not the most important meditation choice you will make.

Eyes

There are two schools of thought here. For some people, meditation is easiest with eyes closed. Closed eyes avoid visual distractions, but can also lead to drowsiness. And closed eyes, because they are not providing any visual input to your mind, can leave more mental room for wandering thoughts.

A better approach is to keep eyes open, with a "soft" focus which isn't intently looking at anything. Your head should remain level, with your eyes cast downward to a point a few feet in front of you. An unfocused gaze provides useful "filler" for your brain which, along with breath counting, helps keep wandering thoughts at bay.

Where to Meditate

You obviously will want to find a quiet location for meditation. If you can set aside a dedicated place for meditation, that is ideal. You may find that concentration is easiest if you sit facing a wall at a distance of a few feet.

When to Meditate

Your own schedule will determine when there is a quiet time in your day for meditation. For many people, first thing in the morning is best because the distractions of the day have not yet started. For others, meditation just before going to sleep brings the day to a satisfying close. Or both. Whatever works for you.

The most important part of "when" is how regularly you meditate. A short meditation period every day is far more effective than one long meditation on the weekend.

Try not to get discouraged or self-critical if (when) you find that you can't always keep to your meditation schedule. Regretting a missed meditation session accomplishes nothing. Neither does making promises to yourself about how you are going to be better in the future about meditating. Just stay focused on what you can do, which is to meditate today.

How Long to Meditate

Start with 5 or 10 minutes per session once a day, and then increase your sitting time at your own pace. Different traditions aim for different lengths of sitting times, ranging from 20 to 40 minutes, or more. Let your mind tell you what is right at whatever stage you find yourself. And you need not lock yourself into keeping the same length of session for all meditations. Again, the most important thing is not how long you meditate, but how regularly and attentively you do so.

You'll need some sort of timer to let you know when the time you've set aside for meditating is over. You are unlikely to be able to judge the passage of time accurately while you are meditating.

You can buy timers especially designed for meditation, but time is time so the extra money for a "meditation timer" probably isn't well spent.

The timer on a smartphone will work, but has the disadvantage of tempting you to check your messages instead of meditating. A kitchen timer will also work, but the ring may be a bit jarring. Your best choice is likely to be a small timer with a soft buzz or ring; there are lots of choices available on the internet. One possibility among many is the Ultrak Silent Count-Up/Down Vibrating Timer, sold on Amazon.

Meditation Accessories

Some people choose to enhance the environment for their meditation with candles, incense, bells, altars, quiet music, robes, etc. Nothing prevents the use of such accessories, and for some people they are helpful. But such external items also can distract from the mental process of meditation. So nothing beyond the basic mat and cushion is essential.

Breath Counting

The very modest level of mental activity required for counting breaths helps to reduce the arrival of wandering thoughts by taking up space in your mind.

> *"It helps to have a focus for your attention, an anchor line to tether you to the present moment and to guide you back when the mind wanders. The breath serves this purpose exceedingly well.... After all, the breath is always here, right under our noses."*
>
> — *Jon Kabat-Zinn*

How to Count Breaths

It will come as no surprise that the essential first step in breath counting is to be aware—mindful—of your breath. Breathe deeply through your nose, with your mouth closed unless you are congested.

Notice both the physical sensation and the sound of air moving through your nostrils as you breathe in and out. Although this may seem to be simply noting the obvious, awareness of the feel and sound of your breathing will be an essential element of your meditation.

"In our daily lives, our attention is dispersed. Our body is in one place, our breath is ignored, and our mind is wandering. As soon as we pay attention to our breath, as we breathe in, these three things – body, breath, and mind – come together. This can happen in just one or two seconds. You come back to yourself."

—   *Thich Nhat Hahn*

In noticing the feel and sound of your breathing, you are not trying to concentrate on your breathing. Rather, you are simply trying to be aware of the sensations of your breath.

The next step may seem deceptively easy, but it isn't. While remaining aware of the sound and feel of your breathing, start counting your breaths as you inhale and exhale.

Count "one" (silently to yourself) as you breathe in, "two" as you breathe out, "three" as you breathe in, etc. When you reach "ten," start again at "one," and keep repeating this cycle throughout your meditation. Be sure, while breathing and counting, that your attention is more on your breath than on the numbers you are counting.

There is nothing magic about counting to ten rather than to some other number, but ten is a number which is used in many meditation traditions and is as good a choice as any.

After a few weeks, you will probably want to streamline the counting slightly by just counting the out breaths. Count the out breaths rather than the in breaths since the out breaths make more sound in your head and so are easier to follow.

> *Be sure, while breathing and counting, that your attention is more on your breath than on the numbers you are counting.*

Because counting is so familiar and relatively effortless, you will probably find that you can all too easily keep counting while your mind wanders. Noticing the feel and sound of your breathing takes up more mental space than counting, so paying primary attention to your breaths rather than to your counting will leave less room in your mind for wandering thoughts.

Not all types of meditation involve breath counting, and some meditators who start with breath counting later drop the counting as they experience fewer wandering thoughts during meditation. But that option is months or years down the road. Even monks who spend their lives meditating may come back to breath counting at times of particular distraction.

So breath counting need not be a meditation kindergarten. It can be a complete practice for a lifetime of fulfilling meditation.

Why Count Breaths?

Why count your breaths rather than, say, counting imaginary sheep?

The most obvious reason for counting breaths (rather than something else) is that you are going to be breathing anyway. So you don't have to imagine anything to count breaths; you just notice what you are already doing.

Also, by noticing the breath you are currently taking, you are directing your attention to something in the immediate present—and away from distracting thoughts about the past or the future.

Beginning Your Meditation

Once you have settled in to whatever sitting or kneeling position you have chosen, and have set your timer, here are four steps to take which will get your meditation off to a good start. Note that these steps work downward from the top of your head to your belly.

1. Begin by imagining that the top of your head is touching an imaginary ceiling. Give your spine a stretch by pressing your head up to slightly raise that imaginary ceiling. Then, after a few seconds, relax a bit to a position which is attentive, but which is neither rigid nor relaxed.

2. Next, notice both the feeling and the sound of your breath going in and out through your nose. Although during meditation your breathing should be at a natural rate, slowing your breathing slightly at the beginning of the meditation will help turn your attention to your breath.

3. Check your posture. Imagine that you are a tree ornament suspended by a string from the middle of your chest. That will bring your shoulders back and your belly forward, for a more sustainable sitting position.

4. Finally, notice your belly moving in and out slightly as you breathe deeply. If your belly isn't moving at all, you aren't breathing deeply enough.

You may be tempted to skip the preliminary steps described above since you generally will want to get started with the substance of your meditation— the breath counting. Resist that temptation. Taking an extra few moments to prepare yourself for each meditation session will be time well spent.

Thoughts During Meditation
(and what to do about them)

"Most of the time, we think we are our thoughts. We forget, or have never noticed, that there's an aspect of our mind that's watching these thoughts arise and pass away. The point of mindfulness [meditation] is to get in touch with that witnessing capacity."

— Sharon Sazlberg

"As you spend more days and weeks with your commitment to practice, it might seem that your mind wanders even more.... The fact is that before you started meditating and trying to develop mindfulness, you weren't aware of how many thoughts you have. Now you are, and that's why there appears to be more of them."

—Pema Chodron

Wandering Thoughts Are Inevitable

Very soon after you begin your meditation—and despite your best intention to focus on your breaths—your mind will wander. Instead of counting your breaths from "one" to "ten," your mind will turn to other thoughts. Get used to such mental wandering during meditation. The arrival in your mind of random thoughts is inevitable since that is how your mind has always worked.

For a very long time, your mind will spend much more time wandering during meditation than following your intent to focus on your breath. That is to be expected.

Gently Push Wandering Thoughts Away

When you find that your mind has wandered away from your breathing—as you repeatedly will—try to avoid regretting that you let your mind drift or promising yourself to do better in the future. That is exactly the kind of past and future narrative thinking which you are learning to leave behind while meditating.

Instead of thinking about the fact that your mind wandered, just focus on the breath you are taking at that moment, which currently is the only real breath there is. The breaths you took earlier and the breaths you expect to take later exist only in your mind.

The Importance of Noticing Wandering Thoughts

As you notice (again and again) during meditation that your mind has wandered, your first reaction is likely to be disappointment that you strayed from your plan to focus on your breathing. But noticing that your mind has wandered is a crucial and entirely positive step. Instead of your usual pattern of passively following whatever thoughts come into your mind, you have exercised control over your thinking—a fundamental goal of meditation—by noticing and then putting aside the wandering thought of that moment.

Noticing that your mind has wandered is a crucial and entirely positive step.

"The moment you realize you've been distracted is the magic moment. It's a chance to be really different, to try a new response – rather than tell yourself you're weak or undisciplined, or give up in frustration, simply let go and begin again.... This act of beginning again is the essential art of the meditation practice."

—Sharon Salzberg

Getting Back to Breath Counting

Once you notice that your mind has wandered, take care to avoid dwelling on that fact. Just mentally step gently away from the current random thought and return to your breath counting, starting again at "one."

A few simple steps will help you get back on track:

— Slow your breathing slightly. Although you will want to return to a normal breathing pace once you get back into the rhythm of breath counting, a slight slowdown in your breathing rate as you return to breath counting will help you re-focus after a mind wander.

— As always during the meditation, be aware of the sound and feel of your breathing. This is the most important step in keeping your mind from wandering.

— Check your posture by imagining that the top of your head is lightly holding up an imaginary ceiling.

Meditation Is a Process, Not an Achievement

Unlike learning how to ride a bicycle, meditation is not a skill to be mastered once and for all. Meditation is a continuous and ongoing process rather than an achievement.

Wandering thoughts will always disrupt your breath counting to some degree during meditation. So you will need to keep getting back on track again and again. That is simply part of the process.

And remember that each time you recognize that your mind has wandered, you are taking a step toward awareness of your thoughts—mindfulness.

Ending Your Meditation

When your timer goes off or, in a group, the leader rings a bell to end the session, don't just stop meditating instantly. At least finish the 1-10 counting sequence you were in (or start a new 1-10 sequence if your mind was wandering at the time).

If you are by yourself, consider taking a minute or two after your session has timed out to do some "extra credit" meditating of at least a couple of 1-10 sequences. You may find that your most focused meditation comes after the end of whatever time you had set.

If you have been meditating while sitting on the floor, you'll want to pay some attention to how you stand up, since getting up from sitting on the floor is not something that most of us are used to doing. After stretching your legs and wiggling your feet, bring your feet together and move them back toward your body. Once you are sure that your legs are not asleep, lean forward, moving the weight of your body over your feet. Put your hands on either side of your feet to brace yourself, and stand up.

Beyond Breath Counting

The breath counting process described in this guide can, as noted, be a complete and powerful basis alone for a lifetime of meditation. But there are many other possible directions for a meditation practice, and there is no shortage of information available about such alternatives: Amazon lists 60,000 books about "meditation," and a Google search of "meditation" yields 80 million entries.

Meditation is an important part of many spiritual and religious traditions, ranging from the Roman Catholic mysticism of Thomas Merton, to the yogic practices of Hindu ascetics, to the monastic rituals of Zen monks. The secular meditation practice described here can, if you choose, serve as a starting point for explorations of such traditions.

In a different direction, there are countless varieties of more elaborate secular meditation practices, including the use of visualizations and mantras, as well as guided meditations in which instructors provide narrative guidance during meditation. An internet search will show many such possibilities. One well-established meditation website, offering (for a small fee) hundreds of hours of guided meditation lessons is www.headspace.com. Other meditation websites include www.calm.com, www.buddhify.com, and www. insighttimer.com.

What to Expect

After meditating regularly for, say, a couple of weeks, you can reasonably ask yourself what effect your practice is having on you.

If you are looking for sudden life transformations or for powerfully dramatic experiences, you are likely to be disappointed. Meditation is not so much about becoming a different person as it is about getting a better perspective on the person you already are.

> *"Meditation is the only intentional, systematic human activity which at bottom is about not trying to improve yourself or get anywhere else, but simply to realize where you already are. Perhaps its value lies precisely in this."*
>
> *—Jon Kabat-Zinn*

Any changes will be subtle, increasing only gradually and fitfully. And the test and value of those changes will come when you feel their impact in your everyday life, not just when you are meditating.

"With meditation practice, slowly over time we find that we are more and more able to stay present in everything we do. We can even do it when we're having a conversation: we stay mindful and present to the person speaking to us, rather than wandering off to what we need to add to our shopping list."

—Pema Chodron

But don't go searching too intensively for the effects of meditation. Such effects will likely elude any focused scrutiny. Just be open to noticing changes in how you experience the realities of your life, regardless of the form those changes take. They will be there.

"The purpose of mediation practice is not enlightenment; it is to pay attention even at unextraordinary times, to be of the present, nothing-but-the-present, to bear this mindfulness of now into each event of ordinary life."

—Peter Matthiessen

"If you continue this simple practice every day you will obtain a wonderful power. Before you attain it, it is something wonderful, but after you obtain it, it is nothing special. It is just you yourself, nothing special."

—Shunryu Suzuki

Sources

Page 3   "Don't just do..." A frequently used variant of the familiar phrase "Don't just sit there. Do something." For example, the variant is the title of a book by Sylvia Boorstein: *Don't Just Do Something, Sit There* (San Francisco: Harper Collins, 1996).

Page 13   "...meditation can help us..." Jack Kornfield, *Meditation for Beginners* (Boulder: Sounds True, 2008, 2004), p. 15.

Page 14   "There are many varieties..." The Dalai Lama. Forward to Joseph Goldstein & Jack Kornfield, *Seeking the Heart of Wisdom: The Path of Insight Meditation* (Boulder: Shambala Publications, Inc., 1987), p. ix.

Page 15   "The incessant stream..." Jon Kabat-Zinn, *Wherever You Go There You Are: Mindfulness Meditation in Everyday Life* (New York: Hachette Books, 1994), p. 9.

Page 17   "The past is already gone..."Taizan Maezumi Roshi, *Appreciate Your Life: The Essence of Zen Practice* (Boston: Shambhala, 2001), p. 17.

Page 19   "In a January 2014 article…" Cited in David Derbyshire, "A meditation on the power of the mind." *The Guardian Weekly*, 07.03.14, p. 34.

Page 19   "Since meditation involves…" Evan Thompson, *Waking, Dreaming, Being: Self and Consciousness in Neuroscience, Meditation, and Philosophy* (New York: Columbia University Press, 2015), p. 55.

Page 20   "A study reported…" Cited in Dan Harris and Jeff Warren, *Meditation for Fidgety Skeptics* (New York: Spiegel & Grau, 2017), p. 5.

Page 20   "Several brain-scan studies…" Sharon Salzberg, *Real Happiness: The Power of Meditation* (New York: Workman Publishing, 2011), p. 26. Used by permission of Workman Publishing Co., Inc., New York. All rights reserved.

Page 20   "The November 2014 issue…" Mariette DiChristina, "Mindful, Medicinal, Malleable and Marketable." *Scientific American*, November 2014, p. 6.

Page 21   "The same Scientific…" Matthieu Ricard, Antoine Lutz and Richard J. Davidson, "Mind of the Meditator." *Scientific American*, November 2014, p. 43.

Page 23   "A frequently cited study..." Matthew A. Killingsworth and Daniel T. Gilbert, "A Wandering Mind Is an Unhappy Mind," *Science* 330, 12 November 2010, p. 932.

Page 24   "What we hope to learn..." *Real Happiness: The Power of Meditation* p. 65. Used by permission.

Page 25   The 30 second experiment is based on: Katsuki Sekida, *A Guide to Zen: Lessons from a Modern Master* (Novato: New World Library, 1975, 2003) (ed. by Marc Allen), pp. 25-30.

Page 73   "It helps to have..." Jon Kabat-Zinn, *Wherever You Go There You Are: Mindfulness Meditation in Everyday Life* (New York: Hachette Books,1994), p. 18.

Page 75   "In our daily lives..." Thich Nhat Hahn, *How To Sit* (Berkeley: Parallax Press, 2014), p. 12. Used with permission of Parallax Press, Berkeley, California, www.parallax.org.

Page 85   "Most of the time..." *Real Happiness: The Power of Meditation*, p. 111. Used by permission.

Page 86   "As you spend more..." Pema Chodron, *How To Meditate: A Practical Guide to Making Friends With Your Mind* (Boulder: Sounds True, 2013), p. 65.

Page 91   "The moment you realize..." *Real Happiness: The Power of Meditation*, p. 49. Used by permission.

Page 103   "Meditation is the only..." *Wherever You Go There You Are: Mindfulness Meditation in Everyday Life*, p. 14.

Page 105   "With meditation practice..." *How To Meditate: A Practical Guide to Making Friends With Your Mind*, p. 144.

Page 107   "The purpose of meditation..." Peter Matthiessen, *The Snow Leopard* (New York: The Viking Press, 1978), p. 249. Used by permission of Viking Books, an imprint of Penguin Publishing Group, a division of Random House, LLC. All rights reserved.

Page 108   "If you continue..." Shunryu Suzuki, *Zen Mind, Beginner's Mind* (Boston: Shambhala, 2006), p. 44.

CPSIA information can be obtained
at www.ICGtesting.com
Printed in the USA
LVHW010829020120
642116LV00006B/18/P